THE INDUSTRIAL
REVOLUTION

ANDREW LANGLEY

Viking

Acknowledgments

The publishers would like to thank David Topliss of the National Maritime Museum, Mr. D. W. Harriss of the Beamish Open Air Museum and Josselin Hill of Quarry Bank Mill; Bill Le Fever, who illustrated the see-through pages and jacket; and the organizations which have given their permission to reproduce the following pictures:

Archiv fur Kunst und Gershichte, Berlin: 8 (top left), 15 (top left), 24 (top left), 37 (center), 39 (top right and right of center) **/The Bettman Archive:** 16 (bottom left), 19 (top right), 27 (bottom left), 34 (top left) **/Bridgeman Art Library, London /Bonhams, London:** 5 (top right), **/Broadlands Trust, Hants:** 43 (bottom left), **/Dr. C. I. Davenport Jones, London:** 7 (top right), **/Hermitage, St. Petersburg:** 4 (top left), **/National Railway Museum, York:** 24 (right of center and bottom right), **/Phillips, The International Fine Art Auctioneers:** 29 (bottom right), **/Private Collection:** 14 (top left), **/Royal College of Surgeons, London:** 37 (right of center), **/University of Dundee:** 38 (right of center), **/By Courtesy of the Board of Trustees of the Victoria and Albert Museum, London:** 30 (top left), 43 (above center) **/e.t. archive:** 11 (bottom right), 15 (bottom left), 26 (bottom left), 44 (top left)**/Mary Evans Picture Library:** 13 (top left and right of center), 19 (bottom right), 29 (top right), 35 (left of center), 36 (top left) **/Vivian Fifield Picture Library:** 10 (top left), 18 (top left and left of center), 21 (bottom right), 35 (bottom right) **/Hulton Deutsch Collection:** 26 (top left), 31 (top right), 32 (bottom left), 43 (top right, right of center and bottom right), 45 (right) **/Image Select/Ann Ronan Collection:** 6 (top left), 9 (bottom right), 15 (top left), 37 (bottom left) **/Peter Newark's Pictures:** 12 (top left), 13 (top right), 20 (bottom), 22 (top), 27 (left of center), 31 (top), 32 (left of center)

Illustrators:
Philip Hood: 8–9, 16, 26, 27, 30–31,
Bill Le Fever: 17, 25, 33, 40
Richard Hook: 46–47
Kevin Madison: 4, 30,
Chris Orr: 6, 7, 23, 45
Richard Berridge: 34, 35, 38, 38–39
Mark Stacey: 6–7, 44, 45
James Field: 4–5, 12–13, 28, 29, 36, 37,
Tony Randall: 9, 10, 11, 14, 15, 18, 20, 21, 24, 42, 43
Wayne Ford: 12
Roger Stewart: 19
John Fox (Arcana): 22–23

VIKING
Published by the Penguin Group
Penguin Books USA Inc., 375 Hudson Street, New York, New York 10014, U.S.A.
Penguin Books Ltd, 27 Wrights Lane, London W8 5TZ, England
Penguin Books Australia Ltd, Ringwood, Victoria, Australia
Penguin Books Canada Ltd, 10 Alcorn Avenue, Toronto, Ontario, Canada M4V 3B2
Penguin Books (N.Z.) Ltd, 182–190 Wairau Road, Auckland 10, New Zealand

Penguin Books Ltd, Registered Offices: Harmondsworth, Middlesex, England

First published in Great Britain by Hamlyn Children's Books,
an imprint of Reed Children's Books, 1994
First published in the United States of America by Viking,
a division of Penguin Books USA Inc., 1994

1 3 5 7 9 10 8 6 4 2

Copyright © Reed International Books Ltd, 1994

Library of Congress Catalog Card Number: 94-60549

ISBN 0-670-85835-8

Printed in Belgium

CONTENTS

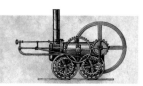

THE WORLD IN 1700

A Dutch windmill for grinding grain. Windmills had been in use in Europe since the early twelfth century. Wind was an important source of power before the Industrial Revolution.

Population, trade, and industry in the eighteenth century.

population per square mile
- ☐ under 50
- ▨ 50 to 100
- ▧ 100 or more

town population
- ■ 500,000+
- ☐ 200,000+
- ○ 100,000+

- ⬭ metal industries
- ≈ wool
- ≋ linen
- ▾ cotton

Three hundred years ago, the world was a much slower and quieter place than it is today. There were big, bustling ports and cities, but the vast majority of people still lived in the countryside. Their lives had altered little since the Middle Ages. Yet in about 1700 a revolution began that was to change these lives dramatically, especially in Europe. We still call it the Industrial Revolution.

TIED TO THE LAND

At this time, more than 90 percent of Europeans lived in rural areas. Most of them worked as peasants on the land, growing their own food and using tools and clothes made locally. The land did not usually belong to them, but to the local landowner. The peasants paid rent, either by working for the owner, or by giving a part of what they grew.

Their lives were simple and often very hard, particularly in times of famine or disease. They had few possessions, and little or no money to spend. Only rarely did they travel far from home, for roads were poor and transport was slow.

FARMING

Farming methods had changed very slowly over the centuries. Many villages in Europe still used the medieval system of strip farming. The fields were divided into strips, which were shared out between the farmers to grow crops.

The system was often wasteful and inefficient. When crops had been grown on a field, it was left for a year to lie fallow, or recover. Geese, sheep, and other livestock grazed on the fallow land — and sometimes wandered into the growing crops as well.

In bad years, the crops would fail and people would go hungry. There might also be too little hay and straw to feed the livestock through the winter. Many of the animals would have to be slaughtered.

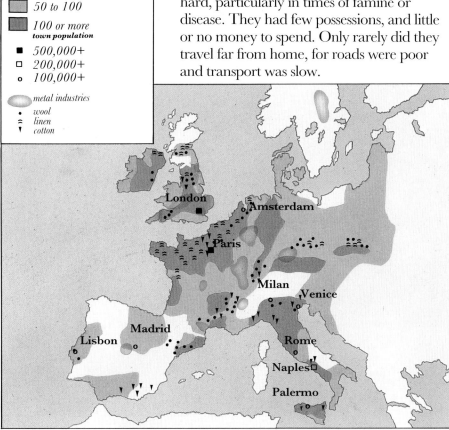

MUSCLE, WIND, AND WATER

The only sources of power in 1700 were natural ones. The muscle power of horses, mules, or oxen pulled plows and carts. Human muscles spread seed, cut firewood, harvested crops, and threshed grain.

The power of the wind and the water was used to turn many kinds of mills. Some ground flour, some pounded cloth, some sawed timber into planks, and some crushed stone. One of the most important uses of windmills was for pumping water out of fields and ditches. These mills drained large areas of farmland in low-lying countries such as the Netherlands.

INDUSTRY

Industry was still run on a small scale. Everyday objects were made by hand by craftsmen such as blacksmiths, carpenters, and wheelwrights. They used few machines, and operated in small workshops in towns and villages. The biggest industries were cloth-making and iron-making. Western Europe had grown rich by weaving cloth for many years, and now raw cotton was being imported for weaving from the Mediterranean and from the American colonies. But there were few cloth factories. Almost all the spinners and weavers worked at home.

The iron industry was growing, too, but suffered from one great problem: fuel. The furnaces were heated by charcoal, made from wood. But charcoal did not get hot enough to make high-quality iron, and supplies of timber were fast running out.

RIPE FOR REVOLUTION

The Industrial Revolution began in Europe, and progressed most quickly of all in England. Why was this?

England was more ready than its neighbors for great change. England had large resources of coal, iron, and other vital materials. It had a good climate, with enough rain and sun to grow crops well. And the size of its population was growing at great speed. All these people needed food — and jobs.

Cloth being woven on a hand-operated loom. The weavers worked at home in their cottages. The wool merchant delivered the yarn and returned later to collect the finished cloth.

Farming had changed little for centuries. Grain crops were still cut and gathered by hand. Farm animals were a random mixture of breeds.

GROWING MORE FOOD

Robert Bakewell (1725–1795) showed how farm livestock could be improved. He bred only from his best animals, and was famous for his Leicester sheep and Dishley cattle.

Between 1700 and 1850, the population of the world began to grow rapidly. This was especially true in the West. Europe's population doubled, and in England the total grew by three times. North America was filling fast, and its population soared from a million to over 26 million.

There were many reasons for this rise, but the most important was food. New ways of farming and new machines enabled farmers to produce much bigger crops. As a result there was enough food to support many more people.

DRILLING AND HARROWING

Since farming began, seeds had been scattered about the fields by hand. The crops that grew were uneven, and a lot of seed was wasted or eaten by birds before it could sprout.

In the early 1700s, Englishman Jethro Tull designed and built a seed drill, which sowed seed directly into the soil in rows. Tull also advised farmers to hoe between the rows frequently. In this way, much seed was saved and weeds and other pests were discouraged. Crops, especially grain crops, grew better and produced a better harvest.

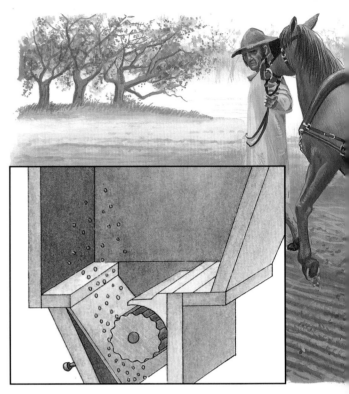

Jethro Tull's drill of 1701 sowed the seeds directly into the soil in rows. This meant that less seed was wasted or eaten by birds. The hopper of the drill (inset) dropped seeds into three trenches at a time.

IMPROVING THE SOIL

The medieval system of rotating crops was simple. A field grew winter grain one year, spring grain the next, and lay fallow for the third. The Dutch were the first to try a new system in which grain was followed by different crops. By about 1650, they no longer had to leave fallow land. They could make it fertile again by spreading manure and by growing clover and new grasses to add nitrogen to the soil.

These ideas soon spread to England, where they were developed by men such as Viscount Townshend of Norfolk. At the heart of his four-course rotation was the humble turnip. After a crop of wheat, turnips were sown, and the land regularly hoed. Sheep or cattle ate the turnips, which were followed by barley and then grass or clover. The rotation of crops and the animal dung kept the land clean and fertile.

Farmland before enclosures (left). The field strips can be seen, and there are areas of woodland and common land. After enclosure (right) these disappear as new hedges and fences divide the land and expand the growing area.

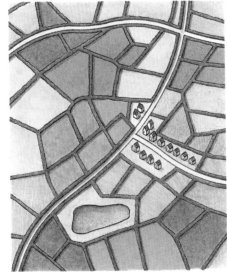

BREEDING BETTER LIVESTOCK

The new system of crops also solved the problem of feeding animals all winter. They could now be fattened on better hay and grain, as well as roots such as turnips.

Since farmers now had more stable herds, they could improve their livestock by careful breeding. Robert Bakewell of England was among the pioneers. He selected animals with the best qualities and bred them together, developing much better breeds of cattle, horses, and sheep.

ENCLOSING THE LAND

English farmers had begun enclosing the open fields in the fifteenth century. Now enclosure became all the rage. Both animals and crops grew better on enclosed land. Between 1760 and 1815, almost 2.5 million acres of land were fenced off.

As a result, many thousands of peasant farmers lost their common land. They were forced to work for other farmers, or to move to the industrial towns.

Pigs like this were bred to grow very large. They were fed on skim milk and whey left over from cheese-making, and on waste potatoes. Fatty bacon was an important source of energy for farm laborers.

NEW AND BETTER CROPS

The opening up of America brought many new crops to Europe. Farmers began to grow potatoes, tomatoes, beans, and corn for the first time. In some areas, such as Ireland, potatoes became the major crop.

The old crops could now be used in new ways. Garden vegetables, notably peas, carrots, turnips, and cabbages, were grown in fields and sold as cash crops for market. Barley and any surplus vegetables were used to fatten cattle and pigs.

Most important of all, farmers started to specialize. In previous centuries, isolated villages had to grow everything they needed — whether the land was suitable for a particular crop or not. Now crops were grown to suit the nature of the soil. Huge quantities of rice were raised in Italy's Po Valley, and wheat on the flat plains of Poland and the Baltic countries.

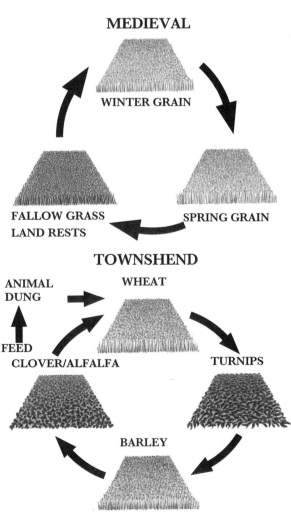

MEDIEVAL

WINTER GRAIN

SPRING GRAIN

FALLOW GRASS
LAND RESTS

TOWNSHEND

ANIMAL DUNG

WHEAT

FEED

CLOVER/ALFALFA

TURNIPS

BARLEY

The medieval system of rotating crops. In the first year, a winter-sown grain crop (wheat, rye, or oats) was grown in the field. Then came a spring-sown crop of barley, peas, or beans. In the third year, the field was dressed in manure and left fallow, or rested, so that it could become fertile again. This meant that one-third of the land lay idle each year. Townshend's four-course rotation system avoided this problem. The wheat crop was followed by turnips, then barley, and then grass or clover for animals to graze on.

7

MACHINES ON LAND

Justus von Liebig (1803–1873) was a German chemist who studied the way plants grow. He proved that better crops could be produced by treating the soil with nitrates and lime.

During the nineteenth century, machines carried on the farming revolution begun by Tull and Townshend. A stream of new implements helped to speed up the improved farming methods, by tilling, harvesting, and carrying things faster and more efficiently. These inventions made it possible for huge areas of land in North America to be cultivated for the first time.

PLOWS
Plows had been used for breaking up the ground for thousands of years. But two new inventions made them much more effective. The first was Robert Ransome's self-sharpening plow, made in England in 1785. Its blades had a soft upper surface that wore away more quickly than the harder base, thus staying sharp.

The second was John Deere's steel plow, invented in the U.S. in 1837. Plain iron

Few effects of machinery are more striking than a steam ploughing engine. Across yonder a curious, shapeless thing, with a man riding upon it, comes jerking forward, tearing its iron teeth deep through the earth.

Richard Jefferies

plows tended to get clogged with mud, but the steel plow stayed clean.

In 1850, steam power was applied to plowing. Fixed to long cables, the plows were pulled across the fields by stationary steam engines.

HARVESTING AND THRESHING
The traditional harvest was a long, slow process needing a huge crowd of workers. The early 1800s saw the invention of several mechanical harvesters by such men as Cyrus McCormick and Obed Hussey in America. A simple kind of combine, which cut and threshed the corn, was developed by 1818.

Thanks to these machines, crops could be cut and stored as swiftly as possible. Steam-powered threshers could separate the grain from the straw, and fans could blow the unwanted chaff away. Grain production

A steam thresher at work. It is operated by a belt from the steam engine. The wheat is loaded in at the top, and the grain is threshed from the chaff, then channeled into sacks.

increased by leaps and bounds. By 1860, there were more than 80,000 mechanical harvesters at work in the Midwest, and the wheat harvest had soared to over 6.5 million tons a year.

DRAINAGE AND FENCING

At this time, scores of new farming tools and machines were invented every year. Many failed and were quickly forgotten, but others played a vital role. Among these was the mole plow, a bullet-shaped plow that was dragged along beneath the earth to cut a drainage channel. The invention of a machine to produce clay drainpipes made the job of draining fields even simpler.

Barbed wire had an enormous impact on cattle farming, especially in the wide open spaces of North America. Wooden fences were expensive, and hedges took too long to grow, but a boundary of barbed wire was cheap and quick to erect. Its main purpose was not, at first, to fence cattle in, but to keep them out of the fields. However, the new boundaries also caused many arguments. Settlers claimed that greedy farmers were fencing off land that did not belong to them.

Steam plows worked best in large, flat fields. The steam engines stood at each end and hauled the plow back and forth on cables. The plow could cut several furrows at once.

FERTILIZERS

Meanwhile, scientists were trying to find ways of making plants grow better. Farmers had been using manure from their own animals for many years without quite knowing what it did. In 1840, the German Justus von Liebig showed the importance of nitrogen and other chemicals found in manure to plant growth. His ideas were taken up in England by Joseph Lawes, who experimented with fertilizers made from bones and minerals.

Soon every progressive farmer was using large amounts of fertilizer. Some of it was guano, a seabird manure imported from Chile: by 1847, British farmers were buying over 300,000 tons of it a year. The rest was "artificial" fertilizer, made in Lawes's new factory near London.

Cyrus McCormick developed his mechanical reaper in 1839. It was pulled by two horses and could cut hay as well as wheat. McCormick founded a factory in Chicago to build his reapers, and showed his invention at the Great Exhibition in London in 1851.

Richard Arkwright (1732–1792) invented the water-driven spinning frame in 1768. He later built a cotton factory in Derbyshire, England, powered entirely by water.

Everyone needs woven cloth — for blankets, curtains, bedsheets, and of course clothing. As the European and American populations grew in the eighteenth century, the demand for cheap cloth grew, too. This led to an astonishing expansion of the spinning and weaving industry. Within one person's lifetime, it changed from small-scale, part-time work for cottagers, into a vast, full-time career for an army of factory hands. This huge change was largely the result of new machinery and new supplies of the vital raw material — cotton.

THE RISE OF COTTON

Textile-making had been an important industry in Europe for many years. Most cloth was made from wool shorn from local sheep herds, spun into yarn, and then woven on hand looms. Smaller amounts of cloth were also made from flax and silk. Nearly all of this labor was done by outworkers, who operated spinning wheels and looms in their own homes.

Cotton first became a serious rival to wool during the seventeenth century. Cotton cloth was brought to Britain and the Netherlands from India. It was cheap, versatile, and very popular, and the wool merchants were worried. In England they were powerful enough to have the import of Indian cloth banned.

The ban turned out to be a disaster for the woolen industry. Businessmen in the north of England began to import raw cotton from the West Indies and Brazil, instead, and turn it into cloth. Very swiftly, cotton production started to catch up with wool.

Until the 1750s, most spinning of thread was done by outworkers in their homes. The threads were spun on a spinning wheel and then wound onto a reel.

The "Spinning Jenny" was invented in 1764 by James Hargreaves. When a worker turned the wheel, spindles pulled and twisted the fibers into threads. One worker using a Jenny could produce as much thread as eight people using a traditional spinning wheel.

FLYING SHUTTLES

Machines were not new to textile production. For centuries there had been spinning devices and fulling mills for beating the cloth. But in the 1770s came a string of inventions that speeded up every part of the process.

First was John Kay's "Flying Shuttle," which dates from the 1730s but was not widely used until later. Up to then, a weaver had to use both hands to pass the shuttle (bearing the thread) from side to side of the loom. This slowed the weaver down. Kay's invention threw the shuttle back automatically, thus doubling the speed of the weaver. However, the weavers and the merchants did not thank Kay for his invention, which they saw as a threat to their livelihoods. A mob broke up Kay's house, and he fled to France.

THE JENNY AND THE MULE

Kay's invention helped both wool weavers and cotton weavers. But, as the amount of imported raw cotton increased, so did the demand for spun thread. The old spinning wheels were much too slow. With one spindle, a worker could produce only a single thread at a time.

The first spinning machines to be driven by water power were made in the 1730s, but were not successful. About 1764, James Hargreaves built his "Spinning Jenny." This was a frame with rows of spindles at each end. Several threads could be spun between the spindles at the same time, greatly increasing the amount one worker could produce. Poor Hargreaves also had his house destroyed by an angry mob of workers.

What's more, the idea for a spinning machine was copied by others. Richard Arkwright's frame was powered by water, and produced a stronger thread. Samuel Crompton's "Mule" made the best thread of all, both strong and fine.

POWER LOOMS

Now that there was plenty of spun thread, the weavers had to work faster. Sure enough, in 1785 the first successful power loom was devised by Edmund Cartwright. It originally needed workers to operate it, but soon became operated by steam. Needless to say, the workers hated the new loom and Cartwright was driven out of business. But his pioneering work made possible the textile boom that was to come.

Many inventors were attacked by mobs who believed that the new machines would make them unemployed. This painting by Ford Madox Brown shows John Kay being driven from his home in 1747.

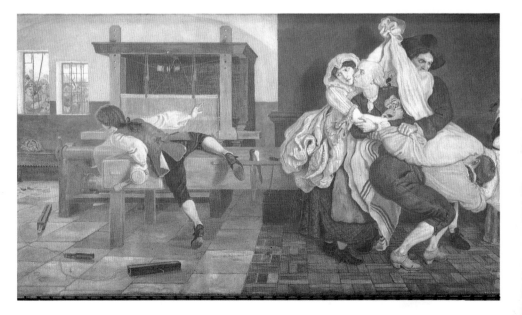

Part of a cotton plant, showing the leaves, flowers, and ripening bolls. When the bolls are ripe, they split open to reveal the seeds and cotton fibers.

The hooks in Whitney's cotton gin combed out the fibers through a mesh and left the seeds behind.

As the cotton industry expanded in the early 1800s, new ports grew up on the banks of rivers such as the Mississippi. The most important were New Orleans and Mobile. From here, bales of clean cotton were taken by steamship to Europe and the North.

By the late 1780s, the textile industry had been transformed. Machines had solved most problems, and could now do nearly everything, from spinning thread to pressing and rolling the finished cloth. The demand for raw cotton soared. But here was another problem. It was simple enough to grow cotton, but difficult to clean the cotton bolls. Once the answer had been found, cotton went on to become the most important product in the world.

WHITNEY'S GIN

In the United States, the South had once grown rich on tobacco and rice — and cheap slave labor. Now the land was exhausted, and slavery was in decline. Cotton farms made little money because it was so hard to separate the long cotton fibers from the green seeds. It took 20 hours of hard work to produce two pounds of cotton.

Then, in 1793, farmer's son Eli Whitney designed his cotton gin. This was a wooden drum stuck with hooks. As it turned, the hooks pulled the cotton fibers through a mesh. The seeds would not fit through the mesh, and fell outside. With this simple machine, Whitney made cotton-growing a big business. Now, a worker could clean fifty times more cotton than before.

SLAVERY IN THE SOUTH

The effect of Whitney's invention was dramatic. Vast new areas of land in the southern states were planted with cotton. British cotton makers, who desperately needed the raw material for their factories, poured money into the new plantations. America's output of cotton shot up from 825 tons in 1790 to over 1.2 million tons in 1860.

The number of slaves increased at the same time from 700,000 to over 4 million. Their lives were miserable. They were forced to work long and hard for no reward, and were poorly housed and fed. Worst of all, they were not free but owned by a white master who could buy or sell them as he chose.

Them days was hell. Babies was snatched from their mother's breast and sold....Chilrens was separated from sisters and brothers and never saw each other agin. Course they cried. You think they not cry when they was sold like cattle?

--- *Female slave* ---

Slaves pick cotton in the hot sun. By 1860, there were 4 million slaves in the South.

FACTORIES AND FARMS

The industry grew up first in the North of England, but soon spread to other countries, despite British laws designed to maintain a monopoly on the new technology. In the 1790s there were many cotton factories in Catalonia, Spain, and in Alsace, France.

Growth was even more rapid in the United States. Samuel Slater, a British textile worker, came to the U.S. in 1789 and designed the first successful spinning mill in America. Other businessmen followed, and large cotton mills sprouted throughout New England. The machines were copied from English models, and powered by water.

THE EFFECTS

The massive growth of the cotton industry brought about many great changes in the societies of Europe and America. Some of these changes were welcome: for the first time in history, clothes, hats, and even shoes could be bought cheaply.

But other changes were for the worse. No longer did rural outworkers spin and weave at home. They were now crowded into factories, part of a large and growing urban workforce.

The most tragic effect of all was the survival, and then the expansion, of slavery in the South. This was to lead directly to the Civil War between 1861 and 1865.

BLEACHING AND SEWING

Meanwhile, many other inventions were helping the textile industry to grow even bigger. In 1785, Claude Berthollet discovered how to bleach cloth with chlorine. Patterns were printed by revolving cylinder presses. Larger and stronger power looms were built.

Equally important was the sewing machine, which was invented, separately, by two Americans named Elias Howe and Isaac Singer in the 1840s. Clothes could now be made quickly and cheaply in factories or in the home.

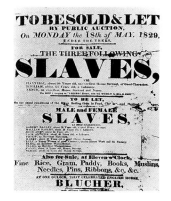

Slaves were bought and sold at auctions. Field hands were usually the cheapest. Skilled workers such as cooks, butlers, and washerwomen might fetch three or four times more.

THE IRONMASTERS

Coalbrookdale in Shropshire, England, was the center of the ironmaking industry. Abraham Darby, his son, and John Wilkinson owned foundries here.

People have been extracting and shaping metal for over 2,000 years. But, even in the late eighteenth century, the iron industry grew much more slowly than the cotton industry.

New machines were not enough; the industry also needed new ways of treating the iron ore to produce a stronger metal. Once these ways were discovered, iron (and later steel) became the essential raw material of the Industrial Revolution. Without it, there would have been no railroads, no big steamships, no large factory machines, and no suspension bridges.

CHARCOAL AND COKE

The traditional way of smelting iron ore was to melt it in a furnace, pour it into molds, and then hammer it into shape. But ordinary fires were not hot enough to burn away all the impurities in the ore. So special blast furnaces were built, which used a blast of air to make the fire much hotter.

For many years, blast furnaces burned charcoal as their fuel, and most ironworks were sited near forests. By the early 1700s the supply of timber for charcoal was running out, especially in England, and coal began to be used instead.

This fuel caused many problems at first. Then, in about 1709, Abraham Darby found that he could bake the coal and turn it into coke. Coke, in turn, produced a better quality of iron. Darby's son later developed a coke-smelting process that improved the iron still further.

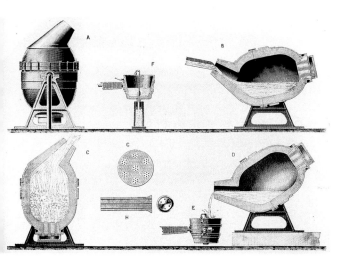

Henry Bessemer built his first iron-to-steel converter in 1856. The huge vessel was filled with molten iron, and air was blown in through the bottom to burn off impurities. The converter was then tipped, and the steel poured off.

PUDDLING AND ROLLING

Iron-making now began to expand in Europe, although Britain still had to buy most of its iron from abroad. But the metal still contained many impurities that could not be burned away in the furnace.

In 1784, Henry Cort devised a way of making a purer kind of iron. The smelted iron was reheated and then stirred with long rods so that the impurites were mixed with air and burned away. This process was called "puddling." Cort also developed heavy rollers that squeezed out more impurities and shaped the iron into bars or sheets.

USES OF IRON

As more iron was produced, more uses were found for it. Plows and other farm implements were made of iron, and so were many of the moving parts for factory machines and steam engines. The first iron bridge was built across the Severn River in Shropshire in 1779.

One of the key figures in the rise of iron-making was John Wilkinson, known as "iron-mad Jack." From his massive furnaces at Coalbrookdale came iron pipes, iron barges, coal-cutting machines, and accurate drills for boring out cannons, rifles, and engine cylinders. Wilkinson was even buried in an iron coffin.

In spite of new smelting processes, foundry workers still had to shift massive weights by hand. Here, they are hauling a hot iron ingot from the furnace to the steam hammer.

THE INDUSTRY GROWS

England was the first country to take advantage of the advances in iron-smelting and working. From being only a small producer in 1750, it had grown by 1850 to the maker of more iron than the rest of the world put together.

Other countries soon followed. At Le Creusot in France, foundries were using coke by 1810. There was a thriving iron industry in Silesia, Germany, by the same time. The United States was slower to take up the new methods, and imported much of its iron from England. It was not until about 1850 that the American iron industry began to catch up.

STEEL

The next dramatic development was the invention of a process for making cast steel. Steel, an alloy of iron and carbon, is much stronger than iron itself. It was traditionally made by heating and hammering iron. Then, in 1740, Benjamin Huntsman made cast steel by heating iron at a very high temperature in small vats called crucibles.

But Huntsman's method was very slow. It was not until the 1850s that two separate ironworkers, Henry Bessemer in England and William Kelly in the U.S., devised a way of injecting air into the molten metal. This converted the iron into steel much more quickly. Soon steel was being used instead of iron in bridges, railroads, metal-framed buildings, guns, and other products.

The world's first cast-iron bridge spanned the Severn River in Shropshire in 1779. Its single arch stretched 120 feet. The parts were cast at nearby Coalbrookdale.

DIGGING FOR COAL

A pit pony is lowered down a shaft in a special harness. The ponies were used to pull coal wagons.

Coal was not a new fuel in the eighteenth century. The Chinese had been burning it for 2,000 years. In Europe, coal had been used in small ovens and workshops since the 1500s. But during the Industrial Revolution it rapidly became the most important of all fuels. It was vital for making iron and for powering the new steam engines. Coal mines brought huge profits for owners, but misery and often death for those who worked in them.

They were about three hundred yards from the shaft when the foul air took fire. In a moment it tore down the wall from end to end, and burning on till it came to the shaft, it then burst, and went off like a large cannon. The men instantly fell on their faces.

— John Wesley —

Small children worked as "trappers" in the pits. They sat for hours in darkness, opening and closing the trap doors to let wagons through.

MINING DANGERS

At first, coal was dug from open pits, but gradually the mines had to go deeper. Shafts were sunk down, and galleries were dug sideways into coal seams. As the shafts went lower, they began to fill with water. Some miners had to work all day with their legs in water. It was not until steam pumps were introduced in the early 1700s that the water could be drained.

There were many other dangers for the miners. Gases might ignite and cause explosions. Shaft ceilings might collapse. Coal dust caused asthma and lung disease. And the work itself was hard, long, and poorly-paid.

GROWING DEMAND

Only one of these dangers was ever greatly lessened. In 1815 Humphrey Davy invented his safety lamp. This had no naked flame to light the underground gases, and was soon widely used in mines.

Unfortunately, Davy's lamp did miners little good in the end. By getting rid of one danger, it encouraged mine owners to go deeper than ever in search of coal, and to open more dangerous shafts.

But, by 1800, the demand for coal was enormous. It was needed in factories and ironworks, and for driving the many new kinds of steam engines. With the invention of railroads and steamships, the demand grew even greater. Between 1770 and 1860, the output of coal in Britain rose from over 6 million tons to over 70 million tons.

CHILDREN IN THE MINES

Coal mines needed huge numbers of workers. While men did the actual cutting, women and children carried the coal up to the surface. Children as young as five or six had to spend all day in the dark, opening and shutting doors to let the coal trucks through.

Pit explosions were common. They were usually caused by coal gases leaking from the seams and being lit by sparks from tools or the flames of candles or lamps.

A COAL MINER'S HOME

A coal miner's house in about 1850. Mining families lived in rows of tiny cottages with mud and cinder tracks in between. Each house had only three rooms, and was home to as many as ten people, who all had to sleep together in two or three beds. The rooms were small and cramped, and often dirty with coal dust. There were no drains and no running water, so clothes had to be washed in the backyard and hung out to dry across the lane behind. The lavatory, behind the house, was shared by several families. Cooking was done on an iron range in the kitchen.

Roof construction

Outside lavatory

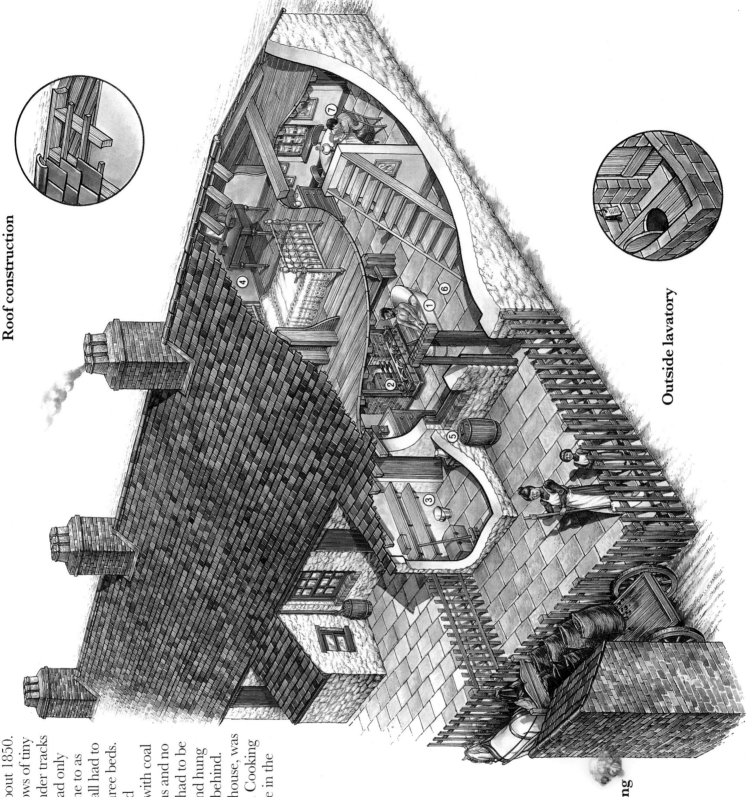

1 Tin bath
2 Iron range for cooking and heating
3 Pantry
4 Slate roof
5 Rainwater barrel
6 Flagstone floor
7 Front parlor

THE POWER OF STEAM

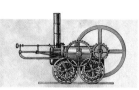

Thomas Savery (1650–1715) was an English engineer. In 1698, he devised the first successful steam pump, which was used to drain water from mines.

The new machines of the industrial age needed a lot of power. The early factories used water and animals to turn mills and capstans. But by the end of the eighteenth century a new and much greater kind of power was being harnessed: steam. Steam engines never got tired like animals. Their only food was coal, which was cheaper than oats or wheat. And they were so strong that one steam engine was able to do the work of hundreds of horses.

HOW STEAM WORKS

For centuries, scientists had been trying to find a way of using steam power. They knew that when water is heated it will expand and turn into steam. If the steam was put into an airtight cylinder and then cooled, it would shrink again into water. A vacuum would be created, which could be used to pull a piston.

This was the theory. But it was not until the development of better iron-working methods that anyone could make a cylinder that was airtight.

SAVERY AND NEWCOMEN

The first person to build a successful steam pump was Thomas Savery, in 1698. His pump had no moving parts, but used the power of the vacuum to drain mineshafts and carry water to gardens and fields. It was very inefficient and slow to work.

In 1712 Thomas Newcomen built another steam pump for mines. This had a large beam whose ends went up and down like a seesaw as the piston below was pushed in and out. Newcomen's machine was safer than Savery's, and used less fuel. By the end of the century, hundreds of Newcomen's engines were at work in Britain and Europe.

JAMES WATT

In 1763, Scotsman James Watt was asked to repair a Newcomen engine. He soon realized that it was a waste of energy to keep heating and cooling the cylinder. So he added a separate chamber called a condenser, where the steam was cooled, or condensed. This allowed the cylinder to stay hot, and saved a great deal of fuel.

Savery's pump had no moving parts. It used the pressure of steam to create a vacuum and suck water upward.

One of the earliest steam vehicles was a carriage built by Nicolas Cugnot in 1769. It crashed on its first trip.

James Watt (1736–1819) improved the steam engine pioneered by Newcomen. He saved energy and cost by condensing the steam in a separate chamber. And he devised a system of gears and cranks that turned a wheel. Later, he added a "governor," which controlled speed.

This new steam engine was completed by 1769. Watt then went on to build a "double-action" engine, which used steam to push the piston as well as pulling it. He also invented a system of cranks to make the pistons turn wheels as well as pushing back and forth. In 1775, he set up a company with Matthew Boulton to manufacture his new engine, which was a huge success.

STEAM AT WORK

As better steam engines were made, more and more uses were found for them. Coal mine owners used them not just to drain water, but also to hoist the coal to the surface. In cotton mills, they were used to power spinning machines and looms. On farms, they were used to haul plows and thresh grain.

Steam also brought great changes to the iron industry. Early steam trip-hammers crushed the iron ore, while other engines worked huge bellows for blasting air into the furnaces. Later, in 1839, came James Nasmyth's mighty steam hammer, which was used for forging iron parts.

By the 1820s steam power was in use all over the world. Paris's water supply was pumped by steam. Sugarcane in Brazil was ground by steam. Flour in Germany was milled by steam. And this was only the beginning of the steam age.

STEAM ON THE MOVE

All the early steam engines were too heavy to be moved about. One of the first to move itself on land was a steam carriage made by Nicolas Cugnot in 1769. This could carry four people for about fifteen minutes before it ran out of steam. It wasn't until about 1804 that an Englishman, Richard Trevithick, built a steam engine that moved on iron rails. Trevithick's engine was lighter because it had no separate condenser and used steam at a high pressure.

Trevithick's steam locomotive "Catch Me Who Can" was put on display in London in 1808. It ran around a circular track at speeds of up to 10 miles/hour.

INVENTIONS GALORE

I ron, coal, and steam — these were the vital ingredients of the early Industrial Revolution. Once they were brought together, there was an explosion of new ideas and machinery. One idea led to another, as engineers and inventors improved on old machines and created new ones. The industries of Europe and America began to pour out products of all kinds.

MACHINE TOOLS

Iron, and later steel, needed new tools to shape them by bending, cutting, hammering, drilling, or grinding. These are called machine tools. The first important machine tool was John Wilkinson's boring mill of 1775. This could cut out cylinders very accurately, and made it possible for efficient steam engines to be built.

Just as important was Henry Maudslay's lathe for cutting screws, devised in 1797. Until then, screws were finished by hand, and were often badly made. Maudslay's lathe produced screws quickly and so precisely that engineers could always be sure that they would fit properly.

This was the great advantage of machine tools. They could produce pieces of work that were exactly the same, time after time. One of the first to realize this was Eli Whitney. After the success of his cotton gin, Whitney opened a gun factory. Here the individual gun parts were made separately by machines and then assembled. This was the beginning of modern mass production.

Samuel Colt built a factory in Hartford, Connecticut, to manufacture pistols with revolving chambers. Colt's revolver was widely used in the Civil War.

Richard Gatling's machine gun could fire 600 rounds a minute. It had several barrels, which were fired in rotation by turning a crank handle.

CANNONS AND REVOLVERS

Whitney's gun factory was soon followed by others. The pioneers of America wanted firearms of all sorts — for hunting, for imposing law and order, and for driving the native Indians from their land. Samuel Colt's repeating pistol, or revolver, of 1835 was the perfect weapon. It had a cylinder that turned after each shot to line up a fresh bullet for firing. Colt also made a repeating rifle.

The effect of the new, fast-action guns was enormous. Colt's revolver was called "the gun that tamed the West." But by the time the Civil War began in 1861, more powerful firearms were needed. An even faster-firing rifle was invented, and Robert Parrot's big new cannon was the first to fire exploding shells. Most deadly of all was Richard Gatling's machine gun of 1862, which could fire 600 rounds a minute.

COMPUTERS

A computer is simply a machine that solves math problems and handles information. The first calculators were invented in the mid-seventeenth century in France and Germany. Then in 1805, Joseph Marie Jacquard built a loom that was controlled by cards punched with holes. The holes caused the needles to pull the thread in a set pattern.

The idea was taken much further by the Englishman Charles Babbage, who spent 40 years working on his "analytical machine." He designed a steam-driven machine that used punch cards to process and store information. But Babbage was ahead of his time. Although he had invented the first proper computer, the engineers of the time were unable to build it.

A painting of the Liverpool docks by Atkinson Grimshaw, showing an early system of gas street lighting. These lights made travel safer after dark and lessened the risk of fire from candles or oil lamps.

Charles Babbage began work on his analytical machine (an early form of computer) in 1834. He also invented the speedometer and the cowcatcher for trains.

GAS AND TAR

Late in the eighteenth century, scientists discovered that coal was not simply a fuel for furnaces. It had other uses. When coal was baked to make coke, it gave out coal gas. Philippe Le Bon in France and William Murdock in Britain showed that this gas could be used for lighting. By the 1840s, the streets of cities as far apart as Birmingham, Paris, and Havana blazed at night under their new gas lights.

Tar was another product of coal. For many years it was thought to be useless, and was thrown away. But people soon began to find uses for coal tar — some of them very surprising. It was turned into dyes, drugs, explosives, and chemical fertilizer. And in 1823 Charles Macintosh mixed a version of coal tar with rubber to make his famous waterproof overcoat.

21

CANALS

A barge being hauled by a horse on the Erie Canal. A horse could pull much greater loads on water than on land. Boatmen had to push the boats through tunnels by lying in the boat and using their legs: there was no room for horses.

The demand for coal and iron grew rapidly during the eighteenth century. As industry expanded, greater loads of these materials had to be carried across country. But coal and iron were heavy, and the roads were poor. One horse could pull less than a ton. However, one horse could pull up to 30 tons of cargo if it was loaded in a canal barge. Water was clearly the answer to industry's transport problems, and in Europe and America huge canal systems were built by the 1820s.

EARLY CANALS

Canals were not a new idea: some had been dug in ancient Egypt and China. The first modern waterway was the Canal du Midi, completed in 1681, linking the Atlantic Ocean with the Mediterranean Sea.

The French canal system so impressed the English Duke of Bridgewater that in 1759 he hired James Brindley to build another. This carried coal from the Duke's mines to Manchester. In 1777, Brindley completed the Grand Trunk Canal, which linked the English ports of Bristol, Hull, and Liverpool.

CANAL MANIA

Canals made a lot of money for the owners. The price of coal fell by half when it began being shifted by water. Over the next fifty years, dozens of canals were built in Britain. By 1800 there were over 4,000 miles of them. Engineers also made rivers wider and deeper so that barges could travel on them.

Canals changed the face of the country. They carried coal and iron to new centers of industry, and stone and gravel for the making of new roads. Other heavy materials, such as timber, grain, slate, and manure, were also transported on the new canals.

> **The canal is little better than a crooked ditch with scarcely the appearance of a hauling path, the horses frequently sliding and staggering in the water, the lines sweeping the gravel into the canal, and the entanglement at the meeting of the boats incessant; while at the locks... crowds of boatmen were always quarreling.**
>
> *Thomas Telford*

Inland waterways were the most important form of heavy transport until the coming of the railroads in the 1820s. They provided trade links between the growing centers of industry.

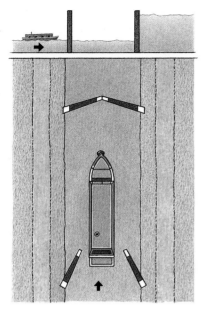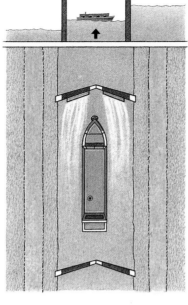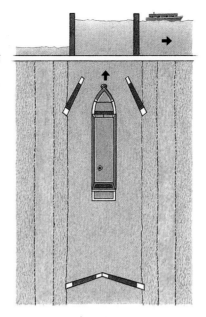

How a lock works:
1. The boat enters the lock and the gates are closed behind it.
2. The sluices in the upper gate are opened and water pours in to fill up the lock, lifting the boat with it.
3. When the lock is full, and the water levels are the same, the upper gate is opened and the boat moves out.

For many years, canal boats were powered by sails. But in inland areas there was often too little wind, so horses were used instead. They were attached to the boat by a harness on a long rope, and walked along the towpath on the canal bank, hauling the boat behind them. The first successful steamboat was built by the American inventor Robert Fulton in France in 1803. After this, many canal boats were driven by steam.

The main difficulty for canal builders was getting boats up and down hills. They overcame it by constructing locks, enclosed chambers designed to lift or lower a canal boat from one level to another.

AMERICAN CANALS

The canal system started much later in the United States. The first canal, at Charleston, was not completed until 1800. In 1825 the Erie Canal opened, allowing cargo ships to sail from the Atlantic Ocean to the Great Lakes. Its success inspired America's own canal mania in the 1830s.

Canals had an even greater effect here than in Europe. Because the land was so much bigger and emptier, long-distance transport was even more vital. The canals brought grain crops from the West to the East, and carried important supplies westward to the settlers of the frontier.

The Erie Canal, completed in 1825, linked the Great Lakes with the Atlantic Ocean. It ran from Lake Erie to the Hudson River, and was so successful that it had to be enlarged several times.

23

George Stephenson's "Rocket" was the most successful locomotive at the Rainhill Trials of 1829. Stephenson won £500 (about $750) and his locomotive was chosen to pull trains on the Liverpool and Manchester Railway.

Thousands of men were employed to dig cuttings and tunnels, and build embankments for the new railroads. Their only tools were picks, spades, and wheelbarrows.

Railroads changed the world more than any other invention of the industrial age. For a start, steam engines were fast. People could now travel more quickly than a galloping horse. Trains could also transport massive amounts of goods over long distances. They carried food to feed the new towns, and raw materials to the centers of industry.

THE FIRST RAILROADS

In the early 1800s, Richard Trevithick built the first successful steam engine that could travel under its own power. Then came George Stephenson, the greatest of the railroad pioneers. His improved steam locomotives were used to haul coal in the mines of northern England.

In 1825 Stephenson completed the world's first public railroad, which linked the coal mines of Darlington with the port of Stockton-on-Tees about 20 miles away. It carried passengers as well as coal, and was an immediate success.

BUILDING NEW LINES

Building thousands of miles of line across unspoiled and often remote country was a gigantic task. Almost all the labor of making cuttings, tunnels, and embankments was done by hand. Armies of men using only picks, shovels, and wheelbarrows changed the face of the land.

The lives of these workers were perilous at best. They worked in harsh conditions, and countless thousands died in rock falls, explosions, and other accidents. They lived together in huge camps and moved across the country as the railway progressed, like an invading force.

The motion is as smooth as possible....I could either have read or written; and as it was I stood up and with my bonnet off drank the air before me....This sensation of flying was quite delightful.

— Fanny Kemble —

A first class railway carriage, spacious and comfortable.

A cheaper "five-a-side" carriage, with crowded, hard seats.

Traveling by train

A passenger's journey began at the railroad station, one of the most splendid buildings of the age. The curved roof was a long canopy of iron and glass, which kept the rain out but allowed fresh air in and smoke and steam out.

There were three kinds of carriage — first, second, and third class. Third class had hard, cramped seats, but was very cheap.

A RAILROAD STATION

1 Iron and glass canopy
2 Broad gauge track
3 Newspaper stand
4 Destination board
5 Ticket collector
6 Station office
7 Ticket office
8 Porter

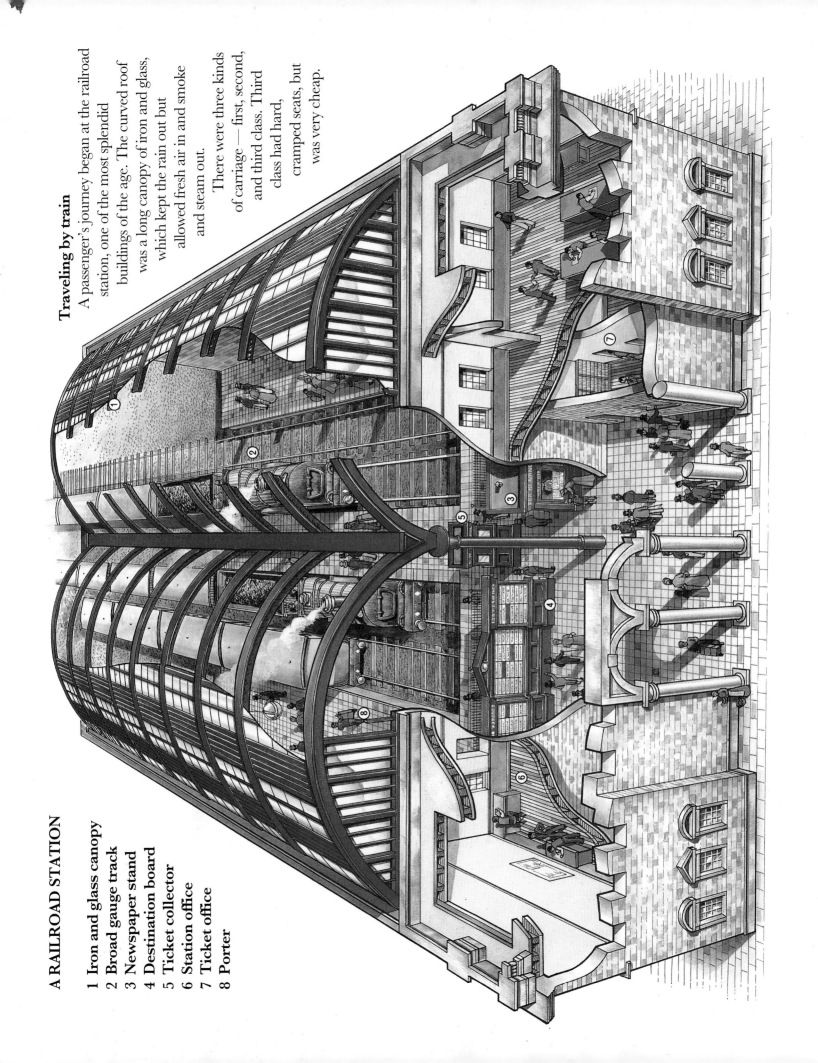

JOINING THE CONTINENTS

Isambard Kingdom Brunel (1805–1859) was the driving force behind the building of the Great Western Railway and the steamships Great Western *and* Great Eastern.

The Great Eastern *was launched in 1858. Its hull was divided into watertight sections. Brunel boasted that it would still float even if cut in two!*

The speed of train travel suddenly made the world seem a smaller place. Journeys that once took days now took only hours. American pioneers were carried from the crowded East to the frontiers of the West. English farmworkers who had never been outside their home villages before could travel all the way to London. Railroads also sped products such as grain and coal from one country or continent to another. Steamships made sea travel faster as well, and new canals shortened journeys further still.

STEAM AND SCREW

Since history began, ships had been driven by oars or sails. The first steam-powered ships were built in the early 1800s by men such as Robert Fulton in the U.S. and Patrick Bell in Scotland. They worked on rivers and short channel crossings, and were mostly propelled by paddle wheels on either side of the hull.

In 1837, Isambard Kingdom Brunel built his ship *Great Western* to take passengers from England to the United States. It was the first all steam-driven ship to cross the Atlantic, and was a huge success. Brunel went on to build two more great steamships. The last of these was the massive *Great Eastern*, which was so big that it could carry enough fuel to take it all the way to Australia. The ship was built of iron, and had screw propellers as well as paddle wheels. Soon, all ocean-going ships were using the new propellers, which were much more efficient in rough seas.

LINKING THE OCEANS

The inland canals could not compete with the faster and more direct railroads. Many canals closed down, and most of the rest made less money. However, even in the 1850s there were plans for new, much bigger waterways. The first was the Suez Canal, which linked the Mediterranean Sea with the Indian Ocean. It opened in 1869, and made the voyage between Europe and the Far East much shorter.

The Panama Canal was an even greater triumph. It took 32 years to build, and was not finished until 1914, when ships could at last sail directly from the Caribbean Sea into the Pacific Ocean. This saved them the huge voyage around South America and through the Magellan Straits. Other important new canals were the Manchester Ship Canal of 1894, and the Kiel Canal of 1895.

RAILS AROUND THE WORLD

Railroads were still the best way of traveling long distances over land, especially in vast countries such as the United States. In the 1860s two companies began work on a railroad to cross the entire continent. One set off from Omaha in the East, the other from California in the West. They met and joined in 1869, forming the Union Pacific Railroad. By the end of the century there were five coast-to-coast lines in the U.S., as well as the Canadian Pacific Railway stretching from Montreal to Vancouver.

Elsewhere, new railroads were bringing far-flung lands into contact with each other. A single line crossed the vast Russian steppes from Moscow to Siberia, while another was built across the Andes Mountains in South America. Major lines were also beginning in Africa and India.

BRIDGES AND TUNNELS

Besides laying tracks, the railroad builders had to build new bridges and dig tunnels.

Two great tunnels, each about 8 miles long, were cut beneath the Alps. In 1882, the first tunnel boring machine began work on a tunnel between England and France. But it soon stopped, because the English feared that the French might use the tunnel to invade.

The modern suspension bridge was invented in 1800 by the American James Finley. Because it was "suspended" over the gap with cables, this type of bridge needed no supports in the middle. The first notable suspension bridge was built by Brunel in England in 1862. Later such bridges include the Brooklyn Bridge in New York, and the Forth Bridge in Scotland.

Work on the Panama Canal began in 1882. It runs 51 miles in length, and took over 30 years to complete. During this time over half a million workers died of disease.

Ferdinand de Lesseps (1805–1894), the French engineer who built the Suez Canal in 1869. He also started the Panama Canal, but went bankrupt before he reached halfway.

On May 10, 1869, railroads built from the East and West coasts met at Promontory Point, Utah. The final rails were fixed with golden spikes, driven in with silver hammers.

27

COUNTRY LIFE

BREAD

CABBAGE

FAT BACON

TEA

A typical meal eaten by a poor country family (above). A wealthy family could expect a much richer and more varied diet (below).

TURTLE SOUP

SALMON

TURBOT & LOBSTER SAUCE

BOILED & ROAST BEEF

GROUSE, CHICKEN, & DUCK

CALF'S HEAD & MUTTON

PLUM PUDDING, TARTS, & JELLIES

WINE

New machines and new methods meant that more food could be produced than ever before. In North America, settlers began growing crops on the Great Plains. But for many country people in Western Europe, life actually grew harder during the nineteenth century. Enclosures had taken away most of the common land where they had once grazed their animals. Instead of working for themselves, they now had to work for the local landowners. If they had no work, they went hungry and homeless.

FARM WORK

Although there were mechanical reapers and threshers, most of the work on the farm was still done by muscle power. Horses remained the most important animals, and the men who tended them were important, too.

Each farm had a large band of laborers who did a wide variety of jobs, from milkers and dairymaids to shepherds and plowboys. At hay time and harvest time, every available hand was needed — even the children were let off school.

The work was long and often very hard. A good harvester with a scythe was able to cut one acre of land a day, even in the blazing sun. Among the worst jobs were hoeing turnip fields and digging out ditches in the depths of winter.

I thought I would get some breakfast, but the poor woman...had not a morsel of either bread or meat. At an inn...a little further on, the landlord had no meat except a little bit of bacon...On the very spot I looked around me and counted more than two thousand fat sheep in the pastures!

— *William Cobbett* —

A farm laborer's cottage was often damp and dirty. Heat came from a stove in the kitchen.

AT HOME

Most farm laborers lived in small houses with only one or two rooms, which they rented from their employer. These contained little furniture, and the floor was often just beaten earth. At the heart of the cottage was the hearth, where all the cooking was done over an open fire, and where the family gathered to keep warm.

RICH AND POOR

Once farming had become big business, land was bought and sold more frequently. And usually it was only the rich — merchants, factory owners, and nobility — who could afford to buy. As a result, most of England and Wales soon belonged to a few wealthy people who lived in great luxury and comfort.

At the other end of the social spectrum were the very poor, who lived in wretched conditions. In England, they were often sent to local workhouses that contained a mixture of paupers, orphans, criminals, and lunatics. The workhouses were crowded, filthy, and dangerous, and earned a reputation as places to avoid at all costs.

THE FRONTIER

In America, the opening of the West was beginning, and settlers by the thousands spread across the country. Prospectors flocked to California after gold was discovered there in 1848. Cattle ranchers and cowboys saw new potential in the "open range" and began grazing herds on the vast grasslands of the Southwest.

Farmers settled on the Great Plains, taking advantage of the Homestead Act of 1862, which gave 160 acres of free land to anyone who could live on the land for five years. Unlike those in Europe, most farmers in America owned their own land and houses, but the work was just as backbreaking and the conditions often more punishing. Neighbors were remote, water was scarce, and pioneers faced brutal winter storms, blazing summer heat, and sometimes even plagues of grasshoppers. In spite of the hardships, many new settlers prospered. The population in the western half of the country grew from less than one percent of the country's total in 1850 to almost 30 percent by 1900.

Life for the poor in a workhouse was harsh and strictly organized. Families were split up, and the food was meager. Men, women, and children were badly treated and made to work extremely hard.

William Hetton Cooke with his wife and children at Worleston Rookery, painted by John E. Ferneley (1781–1860). Very rich country people lived in large houses, with many servants, laborers, and gardeners. Few of them did any work. Instead, they enjoyed themselves riding, shooting, and giving parties.

TOWN LIFE

A boy polishes the shoes of passersby in New York. Many poor children were forced to earn their living on the streets.

Industrial towns grew very fast. Cheap, cramped houses were built for the workers. There were often tall factories and railroad viaducts nearby. These, together with smoke and grime from chimneys, blocked out most of the light.

O ne great change brought about by the Industrial Revolution was the growth of the cities. In England in 1700, only about 15 percent of the population were city-dwellers. Many of these worked as unskilled hands in nearby factories, where they were poorly paid.

THE DRIFT FROM THE LAND

City populations grew so quickly because so many people arrived from the country. The reason for this was simple: machines. New machines and enclosures left fewer jobs on farms, and weavers could no longer compete with machines by doing outwork. At the same time, machines encouraged the building of factories that produced huge quantities of goods. These machines needed people to operate them. Country people flocked to the towns by the thousands, desperate to find work.

HOW THE CITIES GREW

The new industrial towns grew up around the factories, which were usually sited near a river. The tall factory chimneys belched out thick smoke that filled the air and left a layer of dust everywhere. Railroads were built right up to the factories, cutting through roads and walkways. All this work produced piles of waste that were rarely cleared away.

The bigger the town was, the faster it grew. By about 1850, major cities such as London, New York, Chicago, Essen, and Lyons had doubled in size. In the U.S. during the nineteenth century, large towns expanded five times more quickly than the smaller ones.

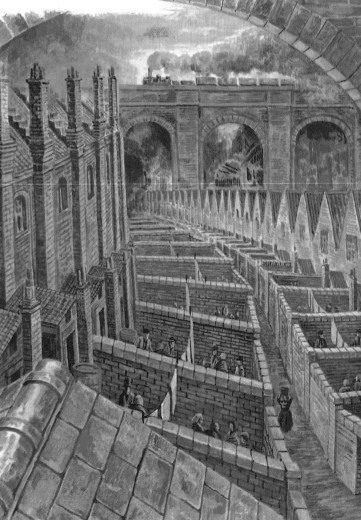

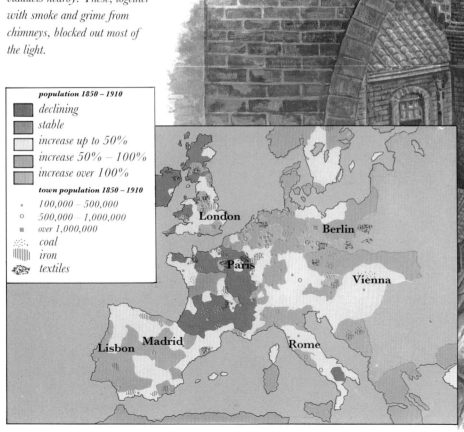

population 1850 – 1910
- declining
- stable
- increase up to 50%
- increase 50% – 100%
- increase over 100%

town population 1850 – 1910
- • 100,000 – 500,000
- ○ 500,000 – 1,000,000
- ■ over 1,000,000
- coal
- iron
- textiles

London
Berlin
Paris
Vienna
Lisbon Madrid Rome

WORKERS' HOUSES

Houses for factory workers were usually built next to the factory itself. There was little public transport, so the workers had to be able to walk to their jobs. The houses were built very cheaply, either in long rows, or as tall apartment blocks. The streets were long and dreary, and there was nowhere for children to play except the narrow alleyways.

With high buildings, viaducts, and chimneys all around, the houses were often sunless and chilly. They were also very crowded, with five or more people sleeping in the same bed. Even the cellars were full — in Liverpool, one in six people lived in a cellar.

STREET CHARACTERS

There were not enough jobs in the factories for everyone. And during hard times factory owners laid off many of their workers. All these people had to find some way of earning a living on the crowded streets.

In 1849, a journalist called Henry Mayhew wrote about the street traders of London and their desperate poverty. He described fruit sellers, flower girls, piemen, clowns, chimney sweeps, and coal porters. At the very bottom of the scale were the sewer rat catchers, the collectors of dog droppings, and the crossing sweepers, who were often small boys. Mayhew's reports shocked the comfortable English middle classes, who preferred to ignore such people.

Ragged children wandered the streets of large cities. Many had no shoes and wore clothes cast off by their parents.

The sewers swarmed with rats. Men were employed to catch the rats, often selling them for dogs' rat-killing contests.

THE BETTER-OFF

Of course, not all townspeople were poor. The factory and mill owners were often very rich, and so were bankers and the merchants who sold the goods. These people did not want to live in the dirty centers of the towns, so they built big houses for themselves on the outskirts.

A few factory owners tried to provide better homes for their workers. In Scotland, Robert Owen improved workers' housing and provided schools for the young children. In the North of England, Titus Salt built a carefully planned community around his mills, complete with a chapel, a school, a hospital, and public baths.

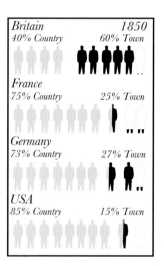

Britain	1850
40% Country	60% Town
France	
75% Country	25% Town
Germany	
73% Country	27% Town
USA	
85% Country	15% Town

Between 1850 and 1870 there was a dramatic population shift from the country to the cities.

Britain	1870
30% Country	70% Town
France	
69% Country	31% Town
Germany	
61% Country	39% Town
USA	
74% Country	26% Town

THE FACTORIES

Spinning mules in Samuel Slater's cotton mill, Massachusetts. The power of water or steam could be harnessed to drive a large number of machines.

Early factories were usually built for ten or twenty people . By the 1850s, a factory might employ hundreds of workers and use scores of different machines. The owner had little contact with any of his workforce — he simply paid them to operate his machines. As a result, factories were often harsh, dull, dirty, and dangerous.

CHILD LABOR

For many centuries, young children had worked on farms and in cities. Because they were smaller and weaker than adults, they were given the simpler and lighter jobs to do. But a child could operate a factory machine just as easily as an adult. So thousands of children, many of them younger than ten years old, were forced to spend long hours in the factories tending the machines. Their parents were eager to send them to work so that they could earn an extra wage. The mill-owners were eager to employ them because they did not have to pay them as much as the adults.

It was a town of machinery and tall chimneys....It had a black canal in it, and a river that ran purple with ill-smelling dye, and vast piles of buildings full of windows where there was a rattling and a trembling all day long, and where the piston of the steam engine worked monotonously up and down.

— Charles Dickens —

Most factory machines were tended by women and children. Because they were small, children were paid less than grown-ups, even though they worked the same hours. Conditions were often dangerous, and there were many accidents.

THE WORKING DAY

Factory workers had a long day — twelve or fourteen hours. Their only day off was Sunday. This was no longer than a weaver might have worked in his cottage. But it was much harder, as the factory hand struggled to keep up with the machines.

There was little time for rest. Most factories had strict rules to keep everyone hard at work, and there were heavy fines for those who missed a day or arrived late. The invention of gas lighting meant the working day could be as long in winter as in summer.

SPREAD OF THE SYSTEM

The first big industrial towns crowded with factories were built in England. In other European countries, the factories were smaller and were usually set away from the cities. Until the 1850s, a great deal of manufacturing work was done in small cottages and workshops.

Factories in the United States developed slowly before the 1830s. This was because the population was widely scattered, and many people had land of their own. Unlike in Europe, there were no hordes of landless laborers looking for work in the towns.

6 a.m.	**7 a.m.**	**9 a.m.**	**1 p.m.**	**8 p.m.**
Get up	Begin work at factory	Short break for breakfast	Break for lunch until 2 p.m.	Finish work and go home

EVERY DAY EXCEPT SUNDAY. PAY: 30 CENTS PER WEEK

A COTTON FACTORY

The textile industry was transformed by the introduction of water-powered machinery. In this factory from the early nineteenth century, the cotton was first carded, to separate the fibers. The fibers were then twisted together on spinning frames to form a thread, which could finally be wound onto bobbins for use. All the machines were driven by a huge waterwheel, via a system of cogs and gears; these were usually very dangerous. Huge belts and wheels whizzed round, but none of these moving parts had safety guards or emergency brakes. The children, because they were small, might have to crawl under the whirring lines of thread to clear blockages or pick up debris. It is hardly surprising that many were killed or seriously injured. Some textile factories provided children with two hours of free schooling a day.

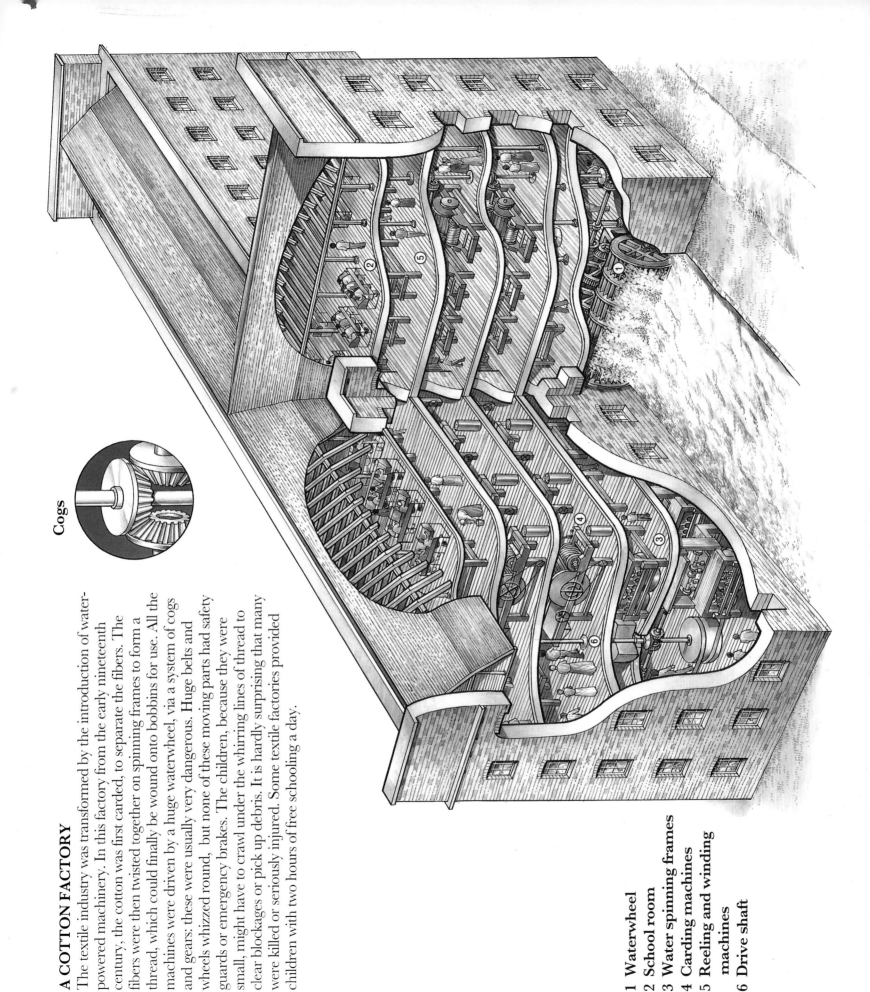

Cogs

1 Waterwheel
2 School room
3 Water spinning frames
4 Carding machines
5 Reeling and winding
   machines
6 Drive shaft

HEALTH AND DISEASE

"Monster soup" — a caricature of what water from the Thames River in London might have looked like under a microscope in 1828. At this time, most drinking water was taken from nearby rivers. These were polluted with filth from sewers and factories and carried germs of disease.

Rich people hired the best doctors to cure their illnesses. They did not go to public hospitals, but were treated at home. Some even had operations at home.

The towns of Europe had never been very clean or healthy places. Now the situation grew far worse. Poor housing, poor diet, overcrowding, and industrial pollution made a deadly mixture, encouraging the rapid spread of disease and decay. Thousands of people died from infectious diseases such as typhus, with little help from doctors or hospitals. Thousands more were crippled or too sick to work.

FILTH FROM FACTORIES

The new factories, mills, and ironworks brought a massive rise in pollution. Steam engines burned coal, which gave off smoke and harmful chemicals such as sulphur dioxide. Iron foundries needed coke, and their furnaces belched out huge amounts of smoke and fumes. Cotton mills polluted rivers with dyes and other waste. Very few factory owners bothered to try controlling this mess.

Conditions were often just as bad in mining areas. Huge slag heaps of waste materials towered beside coal mines and china clay pits. Open cast mines and quarries scarred the landscape for miles around.

BAD HOUSING

We have already seen that the houses of poor people in towns were badly built and overcrowded. They were also very unhealthy places to live. There were no drains or inside lavatories or running water. All the people in one block of houses might have to share three or four outside "privies."

It was almost impossible to keep one's body and clothes clean. Bathtubs and showers were scarcely heard of (even Queen Victoria found to her horror that there was no bathroom in Buckingham Palace in 1837!). Besides which, water had to be brought in buckets from the nearest pump or well. And it was probably dangerous to drink. Until about 1850, most drinking water was taken from the nearest river, which was likely to be polluted with sewage and factory waste.

DISEASE AND DEATH

The filthy streets, the stinking privies, and the foul rivers made a perfect breeding ground for disease. Several epidemics swept across Europe during the first half of the nineteenth century. In 1832, an outbreak of cholera killed many thousands of people — 31,000 in Britain alone. Typhus, smallpox, and dysentery also caused countless deaths.

Besides these terrors, there were lesser diseases, which could also kill. As late as 1894, hundreds of children in London were dying every week from measles. Others were crippled by the effects of poor food.

HOSPITALS

Wealthy people could afford to be treated by doctors in their own homes. The poor could not. They had to depend on charity hospitals, which were founded and supported by gifts from the better-off. There were also sick wards in the larger workhouses for those who had no money.

At first, these hospitals were dirty and overcrowded. Nobody realized the importance of cleanliness and ventilation to get rid of deadly germs. As medical knowledge grew, hospitals became healthier places.

Many people were too poor to pay for medicines and health care. They depended on charity or workhouse hospitals, which were often dirty and crowded.

Artist George Cruikshank drew his picture story "The Bottle" in 1847. It showed how drink could bring ruin to a family (note the coffin in the background). Many working men spent their wages in "gin palaces" and died penniless.

"Death's dispensary." This cartoon from 1866 makes clear that many diseases were spread by unclean drinking water from street pumps and wells. Among the most deadly of these were cholera, typhus, and dysentery.

FOOD AND DRINK

Poor people in the cities usually ate food that was dull and contained few nutrients. Their diet consisted mostly of bread, meat drippings, tea, and thin soup, with a rare treat of bacon or mutton. Country workers were often better off, for they could grow their own vegetables (mainly potatoes).

An even greater problem was alcohol. The "demon drink," gin, was cheap and popular in the 1830s, and caused much suffering. Men spent their meager wages in bars, called "gin palaces," and their families would go hungry.

35

SOCIAL REFORM

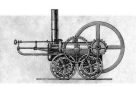

Lord Shaftesbury (1801–1885) led the movement to reform factories and mines in Britain. He encouraged Parliament to pass acts forbidding women and children to work underground, or to clean chimneys.

The plight of the poor eventually caused an outcry. Writers such as Friedrich Engels, Charles Dickens, and Henry Mayhew showed clearly the harsh conditions in which the poor lived and worked. By the 1850s, new laws were being passed and new charities founded, all of which helped to improve the gloomy picture. Scientists and engineers began to make life healthier, too, by providing cleaner water and developing new medicines and treatments.

THE FACTORY ACTS

When the new factories were built, there were no laws about the way workers should be treated. However, in 1802 the British government passed a Factory Act, which limited the number of hours a child could work. In 1819, a second act made it illegal to employ anyone under the age of nine.

These laws failed because crafty employers found ways around them. But in 1833, Lord Shaftesbury launched a series of new Factory Acts. These ensured that factories were regularly inspected, and that guards were put on dangerous machinery. They limited the working day of women and teenagers to 12 hours, and they banned the use of children as chimney sweeps. The Mines Act of 1832 prevented women and young boys from working in the coal mines.

CLEANER CITIES

As the towns of Europe and America grew bigger, the problems of bad drainage and poor water supply grew too. In the 1840s an inquiry showed that more than half of the major towns in Britain had an insufficient or impure water supply. Many people were slow to realize the connection between filth and disease.

In 1842, however, New York became the first large city to have a ready supply of fresh water, which was pumped from many miles away along reservoirs and aqueducts. In England, Edwin Chadwick campaigned for the building of better sewers. By the 1850s, a huge network of pipes and drains supplied London with fresh water and carried waste well away from the city. Major sewage systems were also built in Hamburg and in Paris, after the government had been unable to prevent a cholera epidemic in 1848.

An increasing awareness in public health led to the construction of major sewage systems in many large cities.

MISSIONS AND CHARITIES

Some reformers believed that poor people needed not only better homes and workplaces, but also guidance in their daily lives and behavior. Religious bodies such as the Methodists set up missions in chapels or church halls, where people could meet and talk. In 1878, William Booth founded the Salvation Army in London, to bring the Christian religion to the poor districts. The army soon became active in the United States and Australia as well.

MEDICINE

The Industrial Revolution brought with it a great spread of diseases, but it also brought a surge of medical research. In 1796, the Englishman Edward Jenner discovered that people could be made immune from smallpox if they were vaccinated with the less harmful cowpox. Within a century the deadly disease had all but disappeared.

In 1846, Dr. John Warren used ether as an anesthetic during a surgical operation in the United States. For the first time, surgery could be performed without causing terrible pain. Soon afterwards, the Frenchman Louis Pasteur proved that diseases are spread by

Many people were afraid of Jenner's cowpox vaccine. This famous cartoon (left) by James Gillray shows some of the imaginary side effects of the vaccine.

bacteria, or germs. Joseph Lister used Pasteur's discovery to make surgery in hospitals much safer. He sprayed operating rooms and instruments with carbolic acid, which killed the germs. These and other developments saved millions of lives.

The race that lives in these ruinous cottages, behind broken windows... sprung doors, and rotten door-posts... in measureless filth and stench, penned in as if with a purpose, this race must really have reached the lowest stage of humanity.

--- *Friedrich Engels* ---

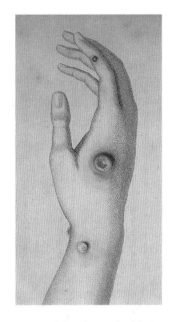

(above) A hand covered with the swellings caused by cowpox. Jenner took samples from these to make his first vaccines against smallpox.

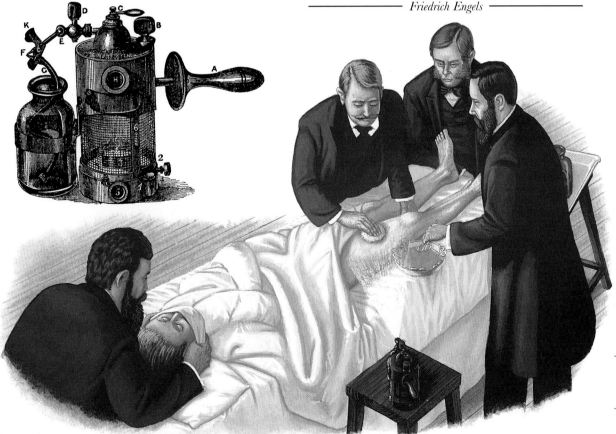

The use of anesthetics such as ether made surgery much less painful during the 1840s. But nearly half of all the patients still died because of infections from germs. Lister's carbolic acid spray (above left) kept wards and instruments free from germs and saved many lives in hospitals.

37

RIOTS AND HUNGER

Thousands of farm workers rioted in southern England and France during the early nineteenth century. They smashed threshing machines, burned haystacks, and attacked landowners to protest the way that machines and enclosures had robbed them of work.

The Industrial Revolution was like a great stone dropped into a pond. It stirred up many societies, and sent ripples all around the world. The landscape was altered, and many lives were changed; some found great wealth, while others found only poverty and hunger. These changes caused considerable popular unrest during the nineteenth century.

In England and France, angry laborers began smashing the new threshing machines, burning stacks of hay and straw, and attacking landowners. The rioting was especially serious in southern England in 1830, where 19 men were executed.

THE GREAT HUNGER

During the 1840s, there was a series of crop failures that caused great hardship in western

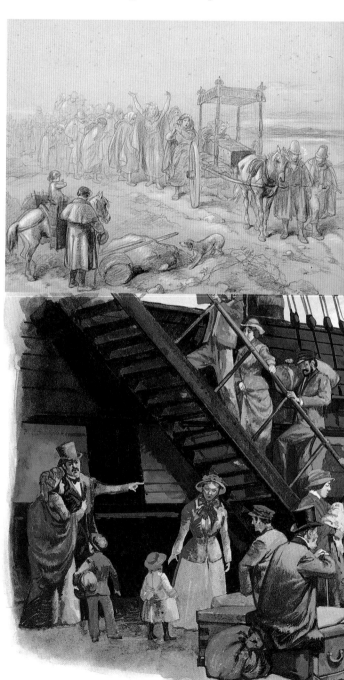

(above right) A victim of the Great Hunger in Ireland is buried in 1845. In a period of five years, nearly a million people died, and many more emigrated.

VIOLENCE IN TOWN

By 1811, the anger of the workers had grown. Mobs roamed the industrial towns of northern England, smashing looms and frames and burning factories. The mobs claimed that they were led by a man called Ned Lud, so they became known as "Luddites." There were similar incidents in Europe. In 1841, a factory of sewing machines in Paris was wrecked by rioters.

RURAL UNREST

In 1815, the long Napoleonic Wars between Britain and France came to an end. Thousands of soldiers left the armies and returned to their villages. But they found there was little work for them. Enclosures and machines on the farms had thrown many out of jobs. Worse still, there had been bad harvests and the price of grain had tumbled.

and eastern Europe. One of the worst hit countries was Russia, where thousands of peasants starved to death.

Even more terrible was the famine that struck Ireland in 1845. At that time, most of the Irish people lived almost entirely on potatoes. A disease called blight ruined most of the year's crop, leaving the Irish with hardly any food at all. The famine continued for five years, during which time nearly one million people died. Two million more left the country to go to England or America.

LABOR UNIONS

Factory and mine owners had a great deal of power over their employees. They decided the wages, and the hours and conditions of work, which were often very harsh. During the eighteenth century, workers made several attempts to form unions that would fight to improve their lot. But governments made laws that forbade the existence of such bodies.

In Britain, labor unions became legal in 1825, but their leaders were often persecuted. In the United States, city-wide labor organizations formed in the 1820s. By the 1870s and 1880s unions had become a powerful force for labor reform in the United States, England, France, and Germany.

THE YEAR OF REVOLUTIONS

The society shaped by the Industrial Revolution was a restless one, and it eventually came to a boil in 1848. The growth of towns, the new speed of transportation, and the widespread movement of people all combined to produce a new interest in politics, often based on the writings of Karl Marx.

The French Revolution sixty years earlier had inspired many people to fight for greater political freedom. Now, populations of several European countries rose in revolt against their masters. There were revolutions in France, Italy, Hungary, Poland, and parts of Germany. Though none was successful, they were the first sign of a break-up in the old Europe.

In 1848 there were rebellions in many parts of Europe. This picture shows troops storming a barricade in Paris.

Karl Marx (1818–1883) argued that war between the working class and the middle class would eventually produce a classless society in which wealth would be shared equally.

Poverty and famine caused over two million people to leave Ireland from the 1840s onward. Many went first to England to look for work, and then emigrated to North America.

IMMIGRANTS

This typical example of a mid-nineteenth century immigrant ship was powered by sail and steam, and could make the journey across the Atlantic in several weeks. First-class passengers ate and slept in comfort, but the journey was extremely arduous for the poorer passengers, crammed together in the steerage, an area below deck.

The poor and hungry of industrial Europe soon began to look overseas for some sign of hope. They found it in the vast and mostly empty countries of the New World, and in the distant colonies of the Pacific. From about 1825, huge numbers of people left their old homes to make a fresh start in the United States, Canada, Latin America, Australia, and New Zealand.

COMING TO AMERICA

Over the next century, no less that 17 million people left Britain and Ireland. Most of these made for America. They were joined by Italians, Germans, Russians, and Poles.

Most immigrants were poor and unskilled workers, but they were also enterprising and adventurous, and they soon got to work on their new lives. There were plenty of jobs in mills, down coal mines, and on the western frontier. Farmland was still

cheap, and the immigrants found that there was land, better food, and clean water.

Some immigrants found jobs on the railroad, especially during the building of the first transcontinental line across America. The Union Pacific company, which started building in the East, hired many Irish laborers. Thousands of Chinese *coolies* (unskilled laborers) worked on the Central Pacific line, which started from the West.

OTHER DESTINATIONS
At the same time, thousands of Europeans from Portugal and Spain arrived in Central and South America, where their home countries had established colonies
Australia's population also soared. The earliest settlers were British convicts who had been transported instead of imprisoned. The first shiploads landed in 1788, but after about 1850, convicts were replaced with voluntary immigrants. Many came in the gold rush of 1851 to seek a quick fortune, but most bought land and took up farming.

Key

1 **Crew's quarters**
2 **Steerage (for poor passengers)**
3 **Storage rooms**
4 **Dining rooms**
5 **First class berths**
6 **Ventilation shaft**
7 **Coal bunkers**

Poorer passengers had no privacy and little room to move or sleep. Most brought their own food, but cooking was difficult and there was much thieving. Water was strictly rationed, and doled out from casks that were often filthy. The poor conditions, added to seasickness and sometimes brutal treatment from the sailors, meant that many immigrants died before they reached land.

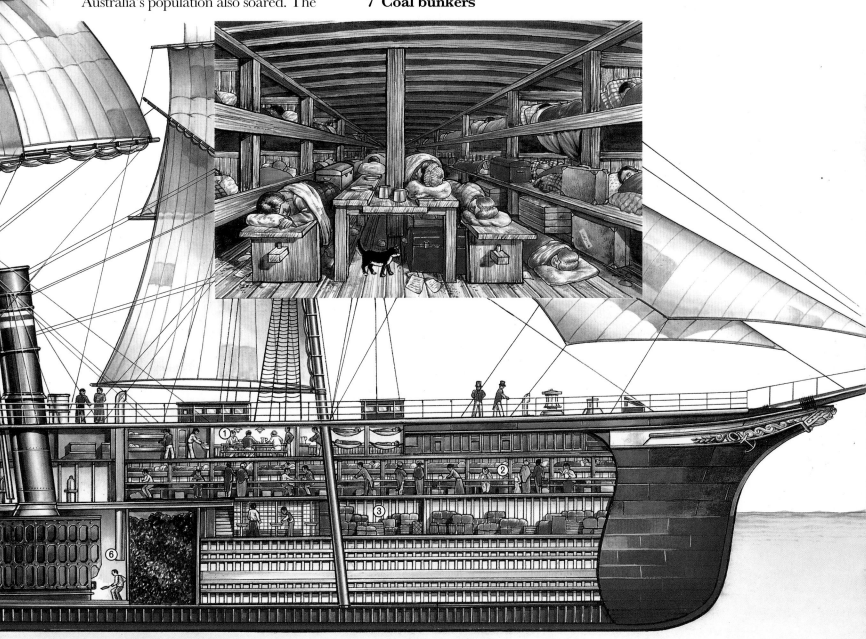

ART AND ARCHITECTURE

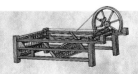

The upheavals of this period directly inspired many artists and writers. But they responded in different ways. Some celebrated the idea of progress, the power and efficiency of the new machines, and the growth of the cities. Others were horrified at the effects of industry, and at the spread of poverty and disease. And there were some who tried to ignore the present altogether, and looked back at a pre-industrial age that seemed more peaceful and civilized.

The Statue of Liberty was a gift from the people of France to the United States. It was first assembled in Paris.

DARK SATANIC MILLS

The English poet William Blake wrote about the "dark, Satanic mills" in his poem *Jerusalem*. These were the factories of the industrial towns, which he saw as works of the Devil.

Many of the novels written by Charles Dickens between the 1830s and the 1860s described another dark place — London. His pen-pictures of the filthy slums, rotten housing, trash heaps, disease-ridden fogs, and neglected paupers shocked many readers at the time. The French writer Victor Hugo also gave a harrowing portrait of the plight of the poor in his book *Les Misérables*, written in 1862.

STEAM AND SPEED

Several writers were fascinated by steam power — especially on the railroads. Never before had they seen anything so fast or so deadly. Many famous deaths in fiction at this time are caused by trains. The heroine of Leo Tolstoy's *Anna Karenina* throws herself under one. In Emile Zola's *The Human Beast* of 1890, the steam train becomes a symbol of evil and greed.

PAINTING A REVOLUTION

New inventions, new ideas, and new landscapes gave painters hundreds of new images to work on. Joseph Wright of Derby depicted industrial scenes, such as a blast furnace by night, or Arkwright's cotton mill. John Constable was inspired by canals and bridges. J.M.W. Turner's *Rain, Steam and Speed* captured the excitement of the new railroads. And the French artist Claude Monet made a series of paintings of the railway station of St. Lazare in Paris.

Strangest of all were the pictures of John Martin, who was enormously popular in the 1830s. He used industrial scenes, such as mines, tunnels, and gasworks, in his illustrations. His painting *The Great Day of His Wrath*, a vision of Judgement Day, was based on what he saw in the industrial north of England.

The Crystal Palace in London was designed by Joseph Paxton and built in 1850 of iron and glass. It housed the Great Exhibition of 1851. The inset shows Paxton's first rough sketch for the palace.

PARADISE LOST

To many people, the new age seemed ugly and heartless. Writers mourned the way in which the beauty and calmness of the landscape had been destroyed, and the way money had become all important. James Fenimore Cooper, the author of *The Last of the Mohicans*, described how the great American wilderness gave way to civilization. Mark Twain's famous novel *Huckleberry Finn* also dealt with this theme.

In Europe, too, the old rural way of life was fast disappearing. English novelists such as Thomas Hardy and George Eliot recorded it in their fiction. Nostalgia for this lost period grew, and soon people really believed that there had been a "golden age" of country living.

MONUMENTS

In previous centuries, people had built cathedrals and churches to the glory of God. Now, they built monuments to the glory of progress and technology. In 1851, a massive cast-iron and glass building, called the Crystal Palace, was erected in London from standardized prefabricated pieces. Inside it was held the Great Exhibition, a display of machines and goods from all over the world.

New materials and techniques meant that giant structures could be built more easily. In 1884 the massive Statue of Liberty, designed by Frédéric Auguste Bartholdi, was placed at the entrance of the New York harbor. In 1889 the Eiffel Tower, made of cast iron, was erected in Paris for the Paris International Exhibition. A triumph of mathematical calculation, the tower was the highest structure ever known.

Three stages of the building of the cast-iron Eiffel Tower in Paris between 1888 and 1889. It contains over 7,000 tons of iron and steel.

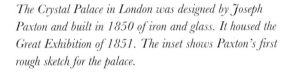

The Iron Forge (left), painted by Joseph Wright of Derby in 1772. Wright was one of the first artists to depict scenes from the new industrial age, including a blast furnace and a cotton mill.

43

NEW KINDS OF POWER

Michael Faraday (1791–1867) was an English scientist who discovered that an electric current could be produced by moving a magnet through a coil of copper wire. Electric motors and generators are based on his findings.

The Industrial Revolution did not stop suddenly, but continued to develop into the twentieth century. Even while the reign of steam power was at its height, scientists were discovering how to make use of electrical power. While railroads were still the main form of transport, the first gasoline-driven cars were being devised. And at the same time, important new machines and processes were being introduced.

ELECTRICITY PIONEERS

People had known a little of the power of electricity for many centuries. Since the Middle Ages, magnetic stones had been used by travelers to point the way to the North.

In the 1740s, American scientist Benjamin Franklin began to experiment with electric currents. In a famous experiment with a kite he proved that lightning is electricity. In the 1790s, the Italian Alessandro Volta built the first battery and produced an electric current. The most important breakthrough came in 1831, when Michael Faraday found that a rotating magnet would generate electricity in a coil of wire. In doing so, he showed that an electric current could be produced by a machine. He also invented the first electric motor.

USING ELECTRICITY

Faraday's invention was soon put to practical use. Larger generators and motors were built. In 1871, the Belgian Zenobe Gramme developed a dynamo, which could generate a reliable and steady supply of electric current. Electricity began to replace steam as the power source for driving factory machinery.

It was discovered that the new source of energy could give light as well. The first successful lightbulbs were developed by Joseph Swan in England in 1878, and by the great American inventor Thomas Edison in 1879. Before long, streets, factories, and even houses were being lit by electricity.

Benjamin Franklin made many experiments with electricity. The most famous of these was in 1752, when he flew a kite in a thunderstorm. Lightning struck a wire on the kite, causing a spark, and proving that lightning was an electric current.

COMMUNICATIONS

Electricity also made it possible for messages to be sent very quickly over long distances. The idea of the telegraph was simple. When an electric current passed along a wire, it caused an iron bar to move, making a tapping sound. A code for these taps was worked out by Samuel Morse, who in 1844 opened the world's first telegraph line, between Washington, D.C., and Baltimore.

Soon there were telegraph lines joining most parts of the world. In 1866, a telegraph cable was even laid across the bed of the Atlantic Ocean between the United States and Britain.

A Scottish scientist named Alexander Graham Bell became fascinated with the telegraph, and tried to devise what he called a "talking telegraph." This was the telephone, which Bell first demonstrated successfully in America in 1876.

THE INVENTORS

The harnessing of electrical power led to a flood of new inventions. We have already seen how Thomas Edison helped in the development of the electric light. In his long life, Edison also produced hundreds of amazing new devices, including the first motion pictures, the stencil copier, the record player, and the tickertape machine. Two other great inventors of the period were Guglielmo Marconi, who made the first successful radio, and Ernst Siemens, who designed the first electric railway engine.

THE WONDERS OF PETROLEUM

Meanwhile, another source of power was being discovered that was to change the face of the world even more than steam. This was petroleum, which had been used in small quantities for centuries. During the 1870s, first lamps and then engines were built that ran on petroleum or its derivative, gasoline.

As the demand for oil grew, wells were drilled in many parts of the world, including the U.S., Russia, Venezuela, and Poland. But soon came an invention that was to make petroleum more important still, and begin a new age of industry. In 1886, Gottlieb Daimler built the first gasoline-powered car.

The first public telegraph message was sent by Samuel Morse in 1844 from Washington to Baltimore. He also invented the Morse Code of long and short taps, which was used to transmit words in a series of electrical impulses.

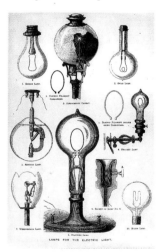

A collection of early lightbulbs. Edison's, with its bamboo filament, is at the top left.

Petroleum was first used for lighting, but quickly became a major fuel for industry and transport. The first big oil wells opened in Pennsylvania in the early 1860s, transforming the landscape.

45

KEY DATES AND GLOSSARY

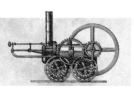

The Industrial Revolution had no definite beginning or end, but developed over more than 200 years. Listed here are the dates of the major inventions and events during that period.

1681 Canal du Midi completed in France
1698 Thomas Savery's steam pump
1701 Jethro Tull's seed drill
1709 Abraham Darby smelts iron with coke
1712 Thomas Newcomen's steam engine
1730 Viscount Townshend develops 4-course crop rotation
1733 John Kay's Flying Shuttle
1745 Robert Bakewell's improved livestock breeding
1752 Benjamin Franklin confirms electric charge in lightning
1760 Enclosures increase in Britain
1764 James Hargreaves's Spinning Jenny
1769 James Watt's improved steam engine
1777 Grand Trunk Canal completed in England
1779 Samuel Crompton's Mule
1784 Henry Cort's puddling process for iron-making
1785 Claude Berthollet's chlorine bleach
1785 Edmund Cartwright's power loom
1786 Gas lights in England and France

1789 First steam-powered cotton mill
1790 U.S. cotton industry begins in Rhode Island
1793 Eli Whitney's cotton gin
1797 Henry Maudslay's screw-cutting lathe
1800 Alessandro Volta's electric cell
1803 Robert Fulton's steamboat
1804 Richard Trevithick's steam locomotive
1810 Friedrich Krupp opens iron works at Essen
1815 Humphry Davy's safety lamp
1825 Erie Canal built. Stockton and Darlington Railway opened by George Stephenson
1831 Michael Faraday discovers electromagnetic induction
1832 Cholera epidemic in Europe
1834 Charles Babbage begins building his mechanical computer.
1835 Great Western Railway begun by engineer I.K.Brunel. Samuel Colt's revolver
1836 John Ericsson's screw propeller
1837 I.K. Brunel's steamship *Great Western* crosses the Atlantic
1842 Joseph Lawes' artificial fertilizer. Massachusetts Supreme Court establishes legality of labor unions
1845 Irish Potato Famine

1848 Karl Marx and Friedrich Engels
publish the *Communist Manifesto*
1851 Great Exhibition in London.
Isaac Singer's sewing machine
1856 Henry Bessemer's steel-making
converter
1859 First U.S. oil well in Pennsylvania
1869 Union Pacific Railroad completed.
Suez Canal completed
1871 Mont Cenis tunnel completed
1874 Barbed wire invented
1879 Thomas Edison's electric light
1885 Karl Benz's internal combustion engine

Glossary

anesthetic: something that causes loss of feeling, and sometimes unconsciousness
chlorine: an element that bleaches and disinfects
cholera: an infectious disease, often deadly
coal seam: a layer of coal between other rocks
cotton boll: the round seed pod of the cotton plant
fallow: farmland left uncultivated
iron ore: rock containing iron and other minerals
lathe: a machine for shaping metal or wood
loom: a machine for weaving cloth from thread
open cast mine: mine dug near the surface
outworkers: spinners and weavers who worked from home, rather than in a factory

paddle steamer: a ship driven by paddle wheels on each side
piston: a disc or rod that fits inside a cylinder and moves back and forth
screw propeller: blades mounted on a turning shaft that drive a boat
suspension bridge: a bridge suspended from cables anchored on each side
transportation: in England, forcible shipment to Australia as a prison sentence
trip hammer: a heavy hammer lifted by a lever and then dropped
typhus: an infectious disease borne by fleas or lice

Quotations

Richard Jefferies (1848–1887) wrote many books about the English countryside. John Wesley (1703–1791) was a traveling preacher who founded Methodism. Thomas Telford (1757–1834) was a Scottish engineer who built bridges and canals. Fanny Kemble (1809–1893) was an English actress. William Cobbett (1763–1835) was a radical politician who wrote books and articles on agriculture. Charles Dickens (1812–1870) became the most famous and influential novelist of his day. Friedrich Engels (1820–1895) was a German who wrote, with Karl Marx, the Communist Manifesto of 1848.

INDEX